vi and Vim Editors
Pocket Reference

SECOND EDITION

vi and Vim Editors
Pocket Reference

Arnold Robbins

O'REILLY®

Beijing · Cambridge · Farnham · Köln · Sebastopol · Tokyo

vi and Vim Editors Pocket Reference, Second Edition
by Arnold Robbins

Copyright © 2011 Arnold Robbins. All rights reserved.
Printed in the United States of America.

Published by O'Reilly Media, Inc., 1005 Gravenstein Highway North, Sebastopol, CA 95472.

O'Reilly books may be purchased for educational, business, or sales promotional use. Online editions are also available for most titles (*http://my.safari booksonline.com*). For more information, contact our corporate/institutional sales department: (800) 998-9938 or *corporate@oreilly.com*.

Editor: Andy Oram
Copyeditor: Amy Thomson
Production Editor: Adam Zaremba
Proofreader: Sada Preisch
Indexer: John Bickelhaupt
Cover Designer: Karen Montgomery
Interior Designer: David Futato
Illustrator: Robert Romano

Printing History:

January 1999:	First Edition.
January 2011:	Second Edition.

ISBN: 978-1-449-39217-8

[LSI]   [2011-06-17]

1308069264

Contents

vi and Vim Editors Pocket Reference

Introduction

This pocket reference is a companion to *Learning the vi and Vim Editors* (*http://oreilly.com/catalog/9780596529833/*), by Arnold Robbins et al. It describes the `vi` command-line options, command-mode commands, `ex` commands and options, regular expressions and the use of the substitute (`s`) command, and other pertinent information for using `vi`.

While retaining coverage of the `vi` clones, `nvi`, `elvis`, and `vile`, this edition offers expanded coverage of the Vim editor, which has become the de facto standard version of `vi` in the GNU/Linux world.

The Solaris version of `vi` served as the "reference" version of the original `vi` for this pocket reference.

Conventions

The following font conventions are used in this book:

`Courier`
> Used for filenames, command names, options, and everything to be typed literally.

Courier Italic
> Used for replaceable text within commands.

Italic
> Used for replaceable text within regular text, Internet URLs, for emphasis, and for new terms when first defined.

[...]
> Identifies optional text; the brackets are not typed.

CTRL-G
> Indicates a keystroke.

Acknowledgments

Thanks to Robert P.J. Day and Elbert Hannah, who reviewed this edition. The production team at O'Reilly Media did a great job helping me make the book look the way I wanted. A special thanks to my editor, Andy Oram, for keeping the project moving with continual gentle encouragement.

Command-Line Options

Command	Action
vi *file*	Invoke vi on *file*
vi *file1 file2*	Invoke vi on files sequentially
view *file*	Invoke vi on *file* in read-only mode
vi -R *file*	Invoke vi on *file* in read-only mode
vi -r *file*	Recover *file* and recent edits after a crash
vi -t *tag*	Look up *tag* and start editing at its definition
vi -w *n*	Set the window size to *n*; useful over a slow connection
vi + *file*	Open *file* at last line
vi +*n file*	Open *file* directly at line number *n*

Command	Action
vi -c *command* *file*	Open *file*, execute *command*, which is usually a search command or line number (POSIX)
vi +/*pattern* *file*	Open *file* directly at *pattern*
ex *file*	Invoke ex on *file*
ex - *file* < *script*	Invoke ex on *file*, taking commands from *script*; suppress informative messages and prompts
ex -s *file* < *script*	Invoke ex on *file*, taking commands from *script*; suppress informative messages and prompts (POSIX)

vi Commands

vi commands are used in "screen" mode (the default), where you use the commands to move around the screen and to perform operations on the text.

Most vi commands follow a general pattern:

    [*command*][*number*]*textobject*

or the equivalent form:

    [*number*][*command*]*textobject*

Movement Commands

vi movement commands distinguish between two kinds of "words." The lowercase commands define a *word* as a contiguous sequence of underscores, letters, and digits. The uppercase commands define a *word* as a contiguous sequence of nonwhitespace characters.

Command	Meaning
Character	
h, j, k, l	Left, down, up, right (←, ↓, ↑, →)
Text	
w, W, b, B	Forward, backward by word
e, E	End of word
), (	Beginning of next, previous sentence
}, {	Beginning of next, previous paragraph
]], [[	Beginning of next, previous section
Lines	
ENTER	First nonblank character of next line
0, $	First, last position of current line
^	First nonblank character of current line
+, -	First nonblank character of next, previous line
n |	Column *n* of current line
H, M, L	Top, middle, last line of screen
n H	*n* (number) of lines after top line
n L	*n* (number) of lines before last line
Scrolling	
CTRL-F, CTRL-B	Scroll forward, backward one screen
CTRL-D, CTRL-U	Scroll down, up one half-screen
CTRL-E, CTRL-Y	Show one more line at bottom, top of window
z ENTER	Reposition line with cursor: to top of screen
z .	Reposition line with cursor: to middle of screen
z -	Reposition line with cursor: to bottom of screen
CTRL-L	Redraw screen (without scrolling)

Command	Meaning
Searches	
/*pattern*	Search forward for *pattern*
?*pattern*	Search backward for *pattern*
n, N	Repeat last search in same, opposite direction
/, ?	Repeat previous search forward, backward
f *x*	Search forward for character *x* in current line
F *x*	Search backward for character *x* in current line
t *x*	Search forward to character before *x* in current line
T *x*	Search backward to character after *x* in current line
;	Repeat previous current-line search
,	Repeat previous current-line search in opposite direction
Line number	
CTRL-G	Display current line number
n G	Move to line number *n*
G	Move to last line in file
: *n*	Move to line *n* in file
Marking position	
m *x*	Mark current position as *x*
` *x*	Move cursor to mark *x* (grave accent)
` `	Return to previous mark or context (two grave accents)
' *x*	Move to beginning of line containing mark *x* (single quote)
' '	Return to beginning of line containing previous mark (two single quotes)

Editing Commands

Command	Action
Insert	
i, a	Insert text before, after cursor
I, A	Insert text before beginning, after end of line
o, O	Open new line for text below, above cursor
Change	
cw	Change word
cc	Change current line
c *motion*	Change text between the cursor and the target of *motion*
C	Change to end of line
r	Replace single character
R	Type over (overwrite) characters
s	Substitute: delete character and insert new text
S	Substitute: delete current line and insert new text
Delete, move	
x	Delete character under cursor
X	Delete character before cursor
dw	Delete word
dd	Delete current line
d *motion*	Delete text between the cursor and the target of *motion*
D	Delete to end of line
p, P	Put deleted text after, before cursor
" *n* p	Put text from delete buffer number *n* after cursor (for last nine deletions)
Yank	
yw	Yank (copy) word

Command	Action
yy	Yank current line
" *a* yy	Yank current line into named buffer *a* (a–z); uppercase names append text
y *motion*	Yank text between the cursor and the target of *motion*
p, P	Put yanked text after, before cursor
" *a* P	Put text from buffer *a* before cursor (a–z)

Other commands

.	Repeat last edit command
u, U	Undo last edit; restore current line
J	Join two lines

ex edit commands

Command	Action
:d	Delete lines
:m	Move lines
:co or :t	Copy lines
:.,$d	Delete from current line to end of file
:30,60m0	Move lines 30 through 60 to top of file
:.,/*pattern*/co$	Copy from current line through line containing *pattern* to end of file

Exit Commands

Command	Meaning
:w	Write (save) file
:w!	Write (save) file, overriding protection
:wq	Write (save) and quit file
:x	Write (save) and quit file
ZZ	Write (save) and quit file
:30,60w *newfile*	Write from line 30 through line 60 as *newfile*
:30,60w>> *file*	Write from line 30 through line 60 and append to *file*

Command	Meaning
:w %.new	Write current buffer named *file* as *file.new*
:q	Quit file
:q!	Quit file, overriding protection
Q	Quit vi and invoke ex
:e file2	Edit *file2* without leaving vi
:n	Edit next file
:e!	Return to version of current file as of time of last write (save)
:e #	Edit alternate file
:vi	Invoke vi editor from ex
:	Invoke one ex command from vi editor
%	Current filename (substitutes into ex command line)
#	Alternate filename (substitutes into ex command line)

Solaris vi Command-Mode Tag Commands

Command	Action
^]	Look up the location of the identifier under the cursor in the tags file and move to that location; if tag stacking is enabled, the current location is automatically pushed onto the tag stack
^T	Return to the previous location in the tag stack, i.e., pop off one element

Buffer Names

Buffer names	Buffer use
1–9	The last nine deletions, from most to least recent
a–z	Named buffers to use as needed; uppercase letters append to the respective buffers

Buffer and Marking Commands

Command	Meaning
`" b command`	Do *command* with buffer *b*
`m x`	Mark current position with *x*
`‘ x`	Move cursor to character marked by *x* (grave accent)
`‘ ‘`	Return to exact position of previous mark or context (two grave accents)
`’ x`	Move cursor to first character of line marked by *x* (single quote)
`’ ’`	Return to beginning of the line of previous mark or context (two single quotes)

Input Mode Shortcuts

vi provides two ways to decrease the amount of typing you have to do: *abbreviations* and *maps*.

Word Abbreviation

`:ab abbr phrase`
> Define *abbr* as an abbreviation for *phrase*.

`:ab`
> List all defined abbreviations.

`:unab abbr`
> Remove definition of *abbr*.

Command and Input Mode Maps

`:map x sequence`
> Define character(s) *x* as a *sequence* of editing commands.

`:unmap x`
> Disable the *sequence* defined for *x*.

`:map`
> List the characters that are currently mapped.

:map! *x sequence*

    Define character(s) *x* as a *sequence* of editing commands or text that will be recognized in insert mode.

:unmap! *x*

    Disable the *sequence* defined for the insert mode map *x*.

:map!

    List the characters that are currently mapped for interpretation in insert mode.

For both command and insert mode maps, the map name *x* can take several forms:

One character

    When you type the character, **vi** executes the associated sequence of commands.

Multiple characters

    All the characters must be typed within one second. The value of **notimeout** changes the behavior.

*n*

    Function key notation: a # followed by a digit *n* represents the sequence of characters sent by the keyboard's function key number *n*.

To enter characters such as Escape (^[) or carriage return (^M), first type CTRL-V (^V).

Executable Buffers

Named buffers provide yet another way to create "macros"—complex command sequences you can repeat with a few keystrokes. Here's how it's done:

1. Type a **vi** command sequence or an **ex** command *preceded by a colon*; return to command mode.

2. Delete the text into a named buffer.

3. Execute the buffer with the **@** command followed by the buffer letter.

The **ex** command **:@***buf-name* works similarly.

Some versions of **vi** treat * identically to @ when used from the **ex** command line. In addition, if the buffer character supplied after the @ or * commands is *, the command is taken from the default (unnamed) buffer.

Automatic Indentation

Enable automatic indentation with the following command:

```
:set autoindent
```

Four special input sequences affect automatic indentation:

^T   Add one level of indentation; typed in insert mode

^D   Remove one level of indentation; typed in insert mode

^ ^D
    Shift the cursor back to the beginning of the line, but only for the current line[*]

0 ^D
    Shift the cursor back to the beginning of the line and reset the current auto-indent level to zero[†]

Two commands can be used for shifting source code:

<<   Shift a line left eight spaces

>>   Shift a line right eight spaces

The default shift is the value of `shiftwidth`, usually eight spaces.

Substitution and Regular Expressions

Regular expressions, and their use with the substitute command, are what give **vi** most of its significant editing power.

---

[*] ^ ^D and 0 ^D are not in **elvis**.

[†] The **nvi** 1.79 documentation has these two commands switched, but the program actually behaves as described here.

The Substitute Command

The general form of the substitute command is:

```
:[addr1[,addr2]]s/old/new/[flags]
```

Omitting the search pattern (:s/*replacement*/) uses the last search or substitution regular expression.

An empty replacement part (:s/*pattern*//) "replaces" the matched text with nothing, effectively deleting it from the line.

Substitution flags

Flag	Meaning
c	Confirm each substitution
g	Change all occurrences of *old* to *new* on each line (globally)
p	Print the line after the change is made

It's often useful to combine the substitute command with the ex global command, :g:

```
:g/Object Oriented/s//Buzzword compliant/g
```

vi Regular Expressions

.   (period) Matches any *single* character except a newline. Remember that spaces are treated as characters.

*   Matches zero or more (as many as there are) of the single character that immediately precedes it.

     The * can follow a metacharacter, such as ., or a range in brackets.

^   When used at the start of a regular expression, ^ requires that the following regular expression be found at the beginning of the line. When not at the beginning of a regular expression, ^ stands for itself.

$ When used at the end of a regular expression, $ requires that the preceding regular expression be found at the end

---

of the line. When not at the end of a regular expression, $ stands for itself.

\   Treats the following special character as an ordinary character. Use \\ to get a literal backslash.

~   Matches whatever regular expression was used in the *last* search.

[ ]

Matches any *one* of the characters enclosed between the brackets. A range of consecutive characters can be specified by separating the first and last characters in the range with a hyphen.

You can include more than one range inside brackets and specify a mix of ranges and separate characters.

Most metacharacters lose their special meaning inside brackets, so you don't need to escape them if you want to use them as ordinary characters. Within brackets, the three metacharacters you still need to escape are \ -]. The hyphen (-) acquires meaning as a range specifier; to use an actual hyphen, you can also place it as the first character inside the brackets.

A caret (^) has special meaning only when it's the first character inside the brackets, but in this case, the meaning differs from that of the normal ^ metacharacter. As the first character within brackets, a ^ reverses their sense: the brackets match any one character *not* in the list. For example, [^a-z] matches any character that's not a lowercase letter.

CAUTION

On modern systems, the *locale* can affect the interpretation of ranges within brackets, causing vi to match letters in a surprising fashion. It is better to use POSIX bracket expressions (see "POSIX Bracket Expressions" on page 14) to match specific kinds of characters, such as all lowercase or all uppercase characters.

`\(...\)`

> Saves the pattern enclosed between `\(` and `\)` into a special holding space or "hold buffer." You can save up to nine patterns in this way on a single line.
>
> You can also use the `\n` notation within a search or substitute string:
>
> ```
> :s/\(abcd\)\1/alphabet-soup/
> ```
>
> changes abcdabcd into alphabet-soup.[‡]

`\<  \>`

> Matches characters at the beginning (`\<`) or end (`\>`) of a word. The end or beginning of a word is determined either by a punctuation mark or by a space. Unlike `\(...\)`, these don't have to be used in matched pairs.

POSIX Bracket Expressions

POSIX bracket expressions may contain the following:

Character classes

> A POSIX character class consists of keywords bracketed by `[:` and `:]`. The keywords describe different classes of characters, such as alphabetic characters, control characters, and so on (see the following table).

Collating symbols

> A collating symbol is a multicharacter sequence that should be treated as a unit. It consists of the characters bracketed by `[.` and `.]`.

Equivalence classes

> An equivalence class lists a set of characters that should be considered equivalent, such as e and è. It consists of a named element from the locale, bracketed by `[=` and `=]`.

All three constructs must appear *inside* the square brackets of a bracket expression.

---

‡ This works with vi, nvi, and Vim, but not with elvis or vile.

POSIX character classes

Class	Matching characters
[:alnum:]	Alphanumeric characters
[:alpha:]	Alphabetic characters
[:blank:]	Space and tab characters
[:cntrl:]	Control characters
[:digit:]	Numeric characters
[:graph:]	Printable and visible (nonspace) characters
[:lower:]	Lowercase characters
[:print:]	Printable characters (includes whitespace)
[:punct:]	Punctuation characters
[:space:]	Whitespace characters
[:upper:]	Uppercase characters
[:xdigit:]	Hexadecimal digits

Metacharacters Used in Replacement Strings

\n Is replaced with the text matched by the *n*th pattern previously saved by \(and \), where *n* is a number from one to nine, and previously saved patterns (kept in hold buffers) are counted from the left on the line.

\ Treats the following special character as an ordinary character. To specify a real backslash, type two in a row (\\).

& Is replaced with the entire text matched by the search pattern when used in a replacement string. This is useful when you want to avoid retyping text.

~ The string found is replaced with the replacement text specified in the last substitute command. This is useful for repeating an edit.

\u *or* \l
    Changes the next character in the replacement string to uppercase or lowercase, respectively.

\U *or* \L *and* \e *or* \E

> \U and \L are similar to \u or \l, but all following charac-
> ters are converted to uppercase or lowercase until the end
> of the replacement string or until \e or \E is reached. If
> there is no \e or \E, all characters of the replacement text
> are affected by the \U or \L.

More Substitution Tricks

- You can instruct **vi** to ignore case by typing `:set ic`.
- A simple `:s` is the same as `:s//~/`.
- `:&` is the same as `:s`. You can follow the **&** with **g** to make
  the substitution globally on the line, and even use it with
  a line range.
- You can use the [&] key as a **vi** command to perform
  the `:&` command, i.e., to repeat the last substitution.
- The `:~` command is similar to the `:&` command, but with
  a subtle difference. The search pattern used is the last regular expression used in *any* command, not necessarily the
  one used in the last substitute command.
- Besides the / character, you may use any nonalphanu-
  meric, nonwhitespace character as your delimiter, except
  backslash, double quote, and the vertical bar (\, ", and |).
- When the **edcompatible** option is enabled, **vi** remembers
  the flags (**g** for global and **c** for confirmation) used on the
  last substitution and applies them to the next one.

ex Commands

This section summarizes the **ex** commands used from the colon
prompt in **vi**.

Command Syntax

    :[*address*] *command* [*options*]

Address Symbols

Address	Includes
1,$	All lines in the file
x,y	Lines x through y
x;y	Lines x through y, with current line reset to x
0	Top of file
.	Current line
n	Absolute line number n
$	Last line
%	All lines; same as 1,$
x-n	n lines before x
x+n	n lines after x
-[n]	One or n lines previous
+[n]	One or n lines ahead
' x	Line marked with x (single quote)
' '	Previous mark (two single quotes)
/pat/ or ?pat?	Ahead or back to the line where *pat* matches

Command Option Symbols

Symbol	Meaning
!	A variant form of the command
count	Repeat the command *count* times
file	Filename: % is current file, # is previous file

Alphabetical List of Commands

The following table of ex commands covers both standard ex commands and selected commands specific to Vim. Commands covered in "Vim—vi Improved" on page 25 are omitted here.

Full name	Command	Vim only
Abbrev	ab [*string text*]	
Append	[*address*] a[!] *text* .	
Args	ar	
Args	args files ...	✓
Bdelete	[*num*] bd[!] [*num*]	✓
Buffer	[*num*] b[!] [*num*]	✓
Buffers	[*num*] buffers[!]	✓
Center	[*address*] ce [*width*]	✓
Change	[*address*]c[!] *text* .	
Chdir	cd *directory*	
Copy	[*address*] co *destination*	
Delete	[*address*] d [*buffer*]	
Edit	e [!][+*n*] [*filename*]	
File	f [*filename*]	
Global	[*address*]g[!]/*pattern*/[*commands*]	
Insert	[*address*]i[!] *text* .	
Join	[*address*]j[!][*count*]	
K (mark)	[*address*] k *char*	
Left	[*address*] le [*count*]	✓
List	[*address*] l [*count*]	
Map	map *char commands*	
Mark	[*address*] ma *char*	
Mkexrc	mk[!] *file*	✓
Move	[*address*] m *destination*	
Next	n[!] [[+*command*] *filelist*]	
Number	[*address*] nu [*count*]	

Full name	Command	Vim only
Open	[address] o [/pattern/]	
Preserve	pre	
Previous	prev[!]	✓
Print	[address] p [count]	
	[address] P [count]	
Put	[address] pu [char]	
Quit	q[!]	
Read	[address] r filename	
Read	[address] r ! command	
Recover	rec [filename]	
Rewind	rew[!]	
Right	[address] ri [count]	✓
Set	set	
	set option	
	set nooption	
	set option=value	
	set option?	
Shell	sh	
Source	so filename	
Stop	st	
Substitute	[addr] s [/pat/repl/][opts]	
Suspend	su	
T (to)	[address]t destination	
Tag	[address] ta tag	
Unabbreviate	una word	
Undo	u	
Unmap	unm char	
V (global exclude)	[address] v/pattern/[commands]	
Version	ve	
Visual	[address] vi [type] [count]	
Visual	vi [+n] [filename]	

Full name	Command	Vim only
Write	[*address*] w[!] [[>>]*filename*]	
Write	[*address*] w !*command*	
Wall (write all)	wa[!]	✓
Wq (write + quit)	wq[!]	
Wqall (write all + quit)	wqa[!]	✓
Xit	x	
Yank	[*address*] y [*char*] [*count*]	
Z (position line)	[*address*] z[*type*] [*count*]	

type can be one of:

+ Place line at the top of the window (default)

- Place line at bottom of the window

. Place line in the center of the window

^ Print the previous window

= Place line in the center of the window and leave the current line at this line

! (execute command)	[*address*] !*command*	
@ (execute register)	[*address*] @ [*char*]	
= (line number)	[*address*] =	
< > (shift)	[*address*] < [*count*] [*address*] > [*count*]	
& (repeat substitute)	[*address*] & [*options*] [*count*]	
~	[*address*]~[*count*]	

Like &, but with last used regular expression; for details, see Chapter 6 of *Learning the vi and Vim Editors*

Return (next line)	ENTER	
Address	*address*	

Initialization

vi performs the following initialization steps:

1. If the EXINIT environment variable exists, execute the commands it contains. Separate multiple commands by a pipe symbol (|).
2. If EXINIT doesn't exist, look for the file $HOME/.exrc. If it exists, read and execute it.
3. If either EXINIT or $HOME/.exrc turns on the exrc option, read and execute the file ./.exrc, if it exists.
4. Execute search or goto commands given with +/*pattern* or +*n* command-line options (POSIX: -c option).

The .exrc files are simple scripts of ex commands; the commands in them don't need a leading colon. You can put comments in your scripts by starting a line with a double quote ("). This is recommended.

Recovery

The commands ex -r or vi -r list any files you can recover. You then use the command:

    $ vi -r *file*

to recover a particular *file*.

Even without a crash, you can force the system to preserve your buffer by using the command :pre (preserve).

vi set Options

Option	Default
autoindent (ai)	noai
autoprint (ap)	ap
autowrite (aw)	noaw

Option	Default
beautify (bf)	nobf
directory (dir)	/tmp
edcompatible	noedcompatible
errorbells (eb)	errorbells
exrc (ex)	noexrc
hardtabs (ht)	8
ignorecase (ic)	noic
lisp	nolisp
list	nolist
magic	magic
mesg	mesg
novice	nonovice
number (nu)	nonu
open	open
optimize (opt)	noopt
paragraphs (para)	IPLPPPQP LIpplpipbp
prompt	prompt
readonly (ro)	noro
redraw (re)	
remap	remap
report	5
scroll	half window
sections (sect)	SHNHH HU
shell (sh)	/bin/sh
shiftwidth (sw)	8
showmatch (sm)	nosm
showmode	noshowmode
slowopen (slow)	
tabstop (ts)	8
taglength (tl)	0

Option	Default
tags	tags /usr/lib/tags
tagstack	tagstack
term	(from $TERM)
terse	noterse
timeout (to)	timeout
ttytype	(from $TERM)
warn	warn
window (w)	
wrapscan (ws)	ws
wrapmargin (wm)	0
writeany (wa)	nowa

Nothing like the Original

For many, many years, the source code to the original vi was unavailable without a Unix source code license. This fact prompted the creation of all of the vi clones described in this reference.

In January 2002, the source code for the original ex and vi became available under an open source license.

This code does not compile "out of the box" on modern systems, and porting it is difficult. Fortunately, the work has already been done. If you would like to use the original, "real" vi, you can download the source code and build it yourself. See *http://ex-vi.sourceforge.net/* for more information.

Enhanced Tags and Tag Stacks

Vim and most of the other vi clones provide enhanced tagging facilities. You can stack locations on a tag stack, and with Exuberant **ctags**, tag more items than just functions.

Exuberant ctags

The "Exuberant ctags" program was written by Darren Hiebert (home page: *http://ctags.sourceforge.net/*). As of this writing, the current version is 5.8.

This enhanced **tags** file format has three tab-separated fields: the tag name (typically an identifier), the source file containing the tag, and the location of the identifier. Extended attributes are placed after a separating ;". Each attribute is separated from the next by a tab character and consists of two colon-separated subfields. The first subfield is a keyword describing the attribute; the second is the actual value.

Extended ctags keywords

Keyword	Meaning
arity	For functions
class	For C++ member functions and variables
enum	For values in an **enum** data type
file	For static tags, i.e., local to the file
function	For local tags
kind	The value is a single letter that indicates the lexical type of the tag
scope	Intended mostly for C++ class member functions
struct	For fields in a **struct**

If the field doesn't contain a colon, it's assumed to be of type **kind**.

Within the value part of each attribute, the backslash, tab, carriage return, and newline characters should be encoded as \\, \t, \r, and \n, respectively.

Solaris vi Tag Stacking

vi provides ex and vi commands for managing the tag stack.

Tag commands—ex

Command	Function
ta[g][!] *tagstring*	Edit the file containing *tagstring* as defined in the tags file
po[p][!]	Pop the tag stack by one element

Tag commands—vi

Command	Function
^]	Look up the location of the identifier under the cursor in the tags file and move to that location; if tag stacking is enabled, the current location is automatically pushed onto the tag stack
^T	Return to the previous location in the tag stack, i.e., pop off one element

Tag management options

Option	Function
taglength, tl	Controls the number of significant characters in a tag to be looked up; the default value of zero indicates that all characters are significant
tags, tagpath	The value is a list of filenames in which to look for tags; the default value is `"tags /usr/lib/tags"`
tagstack	When set to true, vi stacks each location on the tag stack

Vim—vi Improved

Vim is the most powerful and most popular of the vi clones currently in use. It is the default version of vi on most GNU/Linux systems.

Important Command-Line Options

-b   Start in binary mode.

-c *command*
    Execute *command* at startup (POSIX version of the historical +*command*).

-C   Run in **vi** compatibility mode.

-f   For the GUI version, stay in the foreground.

-g   Start the GUI version of Vim, if Vim was compiled with support for the GUI.

-i *viminfo*
    Read the given *viminfo* file for initialization instead of the default *viminfo* file.

-o [*N*]
    Open *N* windows, if given; otherwise, open one window per file.

-O [*N*]
    Like -o, but split the windows vertically.

-n   Don't create a swap file: recovery won't be possible.

-p   Open a new tab for each file named on the command line.

-q *filename*
    Treat *filename* as the "quick fix" file.

-R   Start in read-only mode, setting the **readonly** option.

-s   Enter batch (script) mode. This is only for **ex** and intended for running editing scripts (POSIX version of the historical "–" argument).

-u *vimrc*
    Read the given **.vimrc** file for initialization and skip all other normal initialization steps.

-U *gvimrc*
    Read the given **.gvimrc** file for GUI initialization and skip all other normal GUI initialization steps.

- -y   Enter "easy" mode, which provides more intuitive behavior for beginners.
- -Z   Enter restricted mode (same as having a leading **r** in the name).

Vim Window Management

Vim lets you split the screen into multiple windows and control their size and placement.

Window management commands—ex

Command	Function
clo[se][!]	Close the current window; behavior affected by the hidden option
hid[e]	Close the current window, if it's not the last one on the screen
[N]new [position] [file]	Create a new window, editing an empty buffer
on[ly]	Make this window the only one on the screen
qa[ll][!]	Exit Vim
q[uit][!]	Quit the current window (exit if given in the last window)
res[ize] [±n]	Increase or decrease the current window height by n
res[ize] [n]	Set the current window height to n if supplied; otherwise, set it to the largest size possible without hiding the other windows
[N]sn[ext]	Split the window and move to the next file in the argument list, or to the Nth file if a count is supplied
[N]sp[lit] [position] [file]	Split the current window in half

Command	Function
sta[g] [*tagname*]	Split the window and run the :tag command as appropriate in the new window
[*N*]sv[iew] [*position*] *file*	Same as :split, but set the readonly option for the buffer
wa[ll][!]	Write all modified buffers that have filenames
wqa[ll][!]	Write all changed buffers and exit
xa[ll][!]	Same as wqall

Window management commands—vi

Command	Function
^W s ^W S ^W ^S	Same as :split without a *file* argument; ^W ^S may not work on all terminals.
^W n ^W ^N	Same as :new without a *file* argument.
^W ^ ^W ^^	Perform :split #, split the window, and edit the alternate file.
^W q ^W ^Q	Same as the :quit command; ^W ^Q may not work on all terminals.
^W c	Same as the :close command.
^W o ^W ^O	Same as the :only command.
^W ↓ ^W j ^W ^J	Move cursor to *n*th window below the current one.
^W ↑ ^W k ^W ^K	Move cursor to *n*th window above the current one.
^W w ^W ^W	With *count*, go to *n*th window; otherwise, move to the window below the current one. If in the bottom window, move to the top one.

Command	Function
^W W	With *count*, go to *n*th window; otherwise, move to window above the current one. If in the top window, move to the bottom one.
^W t ^W ^T	Move the cursor to the top window.
^W b ^W ^B	Move the cursor to the bottom window.
^W p ^W ^P	Go to the most recently accessed (previous) window.
^W r ^W ^R	Rotate all the windows downward; the cursor stays in the same window.
^W R	Rotate all the windows upward; the cursor stays in the same window.
^W x ^W ^X	Without *count*, exchange the current window with the next one; if there is no next window, exchange with the previous window. With *count*, exchange the current window with the *n*th window (first window is one; the cursor is put in the other window).
^W =	Make all windows the same height.
^W -	Decrease current window height.
^W +	Increase current window height.
^W _ ^W ^_	Set the current window size to the value given in a preceding count.
z *N* ENTER	Set the current window height to *N*.
^W] ^W ^]	Split the current window; in the new upper window, use the identifier under the cursor as a tag and go to it.
^W f ^W ^F	Split the current window and edit the filename under the cursor in the new window.
^W i ^W ^I	Open a new window; move the cursor to the first line that matches the keyword under the cursor.
^W d ^W ^D	Open a new window; move the cursor to the macro definition that contains the keyword under the cursor.

Tabbed Editing

Similar to modern web browsers, Vim lets you create and manage multiple *tabs*. Within each tab, there can be multiple windows. You can then switch back and forth between tabs. This is an easy way to work on multiple unrelated editing tasks without cluttering up your screen. Tabs are supported in both the character and the GUI versions of Vim.

Managing tabs—ex

Tabs are numbered from one.

Command	Function
[count] tab command	Run command, but open a new tab when otherwise a new window would be opened, e.g., use :tab split to split the current buffer into a new tab.
tabc[lose][!] [count]	Close the current tab page. With count, close the page whose number is indicated in count. Use ! to force closing, even if file contents have not been saved (the buffer's contents are not lost).
tabdo command	Execute command for each tab.
tabe[dit] [option] [command] [file]	Open a new page with a window editing file. With no arguments, open an empty page.
tabf[ind] [option] [command] file	Open a new page and search for file in the value of the path option, like :find.
tabf[irst]	Move to the first tab.
tabl[ast]	Move to the last tab.
tabm[ove] [N]	Move the current tab page to after tab page N (change the ordering of the tab pages themselves, not which tab you're working in). With no argument,

Command	Function
	make the current tab become the last one.
tabnew [option] [command] [file]	Same as :tabedit.
tabn[ext] [count]	Move to next tab, or to tab count.
tabN[ext] [count]	Same as :tabprevious.
tabo[nly][!]	Close all other tab pages.
tabp[revious] [count]	Move to previous tab, or go back count tabs. This wraps around.
tabr[ewind]	Move to the first tab (same as :tabfirst).

Managing tabs—vi

The control sequences work in both command mode and insert mode.

Command	Function
gt CTRL Page Down	Same as :tabnext
gT CTRL Page Up	Same as :tabprevious
^W gf	Edit the filename under the cursor in a new tab page
^W gF	Edit the filename under the cursor in a new tab page, starting at the line number following the filename

Tabbed editing options

Option	Default
t:cmdheight (t:ch) (per tab page)	1
guitablabel (gtl)	
guitabtooltip (gtt)	
showtabline (stal)	1
tabline (tal)	
tabpagemax (tpm)	10

Vim Extended Regular Expressions

\| Indicates alternation.

\+   Matches one or more of the preceding regular expressions.

\=   Matches zero or one of the preceding regular expressions.

\{...\}

Defines an *interval expression*. Interval expressions describe counted numbers of repetitions. In the following description, *n* and *m* represent integer constants:

\{*n*\}   Matches exactly *n* repetitions of the previous regular expression.

\{*n*,\}   Matches *n* or more repetitions of the previous regular expression, as many as possible.

\{*n*,*m*\} Matches *n* to *m* repetitions.

For Vim, *n* and *m* can range from 0 to 32,000. Vim requires the backslash only on the { and not on the }. Vim extends traditional interval expressions with additional matching notations, as follows:

\{,*m*\}   Matches 0 to *m* of the preceding regular expression, as much as possible.

\{\}   Matches 0 or more of the preceding regular expressions, as much as possible (same as *).

\{-*n*,*m*\} Matches *n* to *m* of the preceding regular expression, as few as possible.

\{-*n*\}   Matches *n* of the preceding regular expression.

\{-*n*,\}   Matches at least *n* of the preceding regular expression, as few as possible.

\{-,*m*\}   Matches 0 to *m* of the preceding regular expression, as few as possible.

\i   Matches any identifier character, as defined by the **isident** option.

\I   Like \i, excluding digits.

\k	Matches any keyword character, as defined by the `iskeyword` option.
\K	Like \k, excluding digits.
\f	Matches any filename character, as defined by the `isfname` option.
\F	Like \f, excluding digits.
\p	Matches any printable character, as defined by the `isprint` option.
\P	Like \p, excluding digits.
\s	Matches a whitespace character (exactly a space or tab).
\S	Matches anything that isn't a space or a tab.
\b	Backspace.
\e	Escape.
\r	Carriage return.
\t	Tab.
\n	Matches the end of line.
~	Matches the last given substitute (i.e., replacement) string.
\(...\)	Provides grouping for *, \+, and \=, as well as making matched subtexts available in the replacement part of a substitute command (\1, \2, etc.).
\1	Matches the same string that was matched by the first subexpression in \(and \). \2, \3, and so on, may be used to represent the second, third, and so forth subexpressions.

The `isident`, `iskeyword`, `isfname`, and `isprint` options define the characters that appear in identifiers, keywords, and filenames, and that are printable, respectively.

Command-Line History and Completion

Vim keeps a history of **ex** commands that you have issued. You can recall and edit commands from that history and use the completion facilities to save typing when entering commands.

History commands—vi

Key	Meaning
↑, ↓	Move up (previous), down (more recent) in the history
←, →	Move left, right on the recalled line
INS	Toggle insert/overstrike mode; default is insert mode
BACKSPACE	Delete characters
SHIFT or CONTROL combined with ← or →	Move left or right one word at a time
^B or HOME	Move to the beginning of the command line
^E or END	Move to the end of the command line

If Vim is in **vi** compatibility mode, ESC acts likes ENTER and executes the command. When **vi** compatibility is turned off, ESC exits the command line without executing anything.

The **wildchar** option contains the character you type when you want Vim to do a completion. The default value is the tab character. You can use completion for the following:

Command names
　　Available at the start of the command line.

Tag values
　　After you've typed :**tag**.

Filenames
　　When typing a command that takes a filename argument (see :**help suffixes** for details).

Option values
> When entering a :set command, for both option names and their values.

Completion commands—vi

Command	Function
^A	Insert all names that match the pattern
^D	List the names that match the pattern; for filenames, directories are highlighted
^L	If there is exactly one match, insert it; otherwise, expand to the longest common prefix of the multiple matches
^N	Go to next of multiple wildchar matches, if any; otherwise, recall more recent history line
^P	Go to previous of multiple wildchar matches, if any; otherwise, recall older history line
Value of wildchar	(Default: tab) Perform a match, inserting the generated text; pressing TAB successively cycles among all the matches

Tag Stacks

Vim provides ex and vi commands for managing the tag stack.

Tag commands—ex

Command	Function
[*count*]po[p][!]	Pop a cursor position off the stack, restoring the cursor to its previous position
sts[elect][!] [*tagstring*]	Like tselect, but split the window for the selected tag
ta[g][!] [*tagstring*]	Edit the file containing *tagstring* as defined in the tags file
[*N*]ta[g][!]	Jump to the Nth newer entry in the tag stack

Command	Function
`tags`	Display the contents of the tag stack
`tl[ast][!]`	Jump to the last matching tag
`[N]tn[ext][!]`	Jump to the Nth next matching tag (default one)
`[N]tN[ext][!]`	Same as `tprevious`
`[N]tp[revious][!]`	Jump to the Nth previous matching tag (default one)
`[N]tr[ewind][!]`	Jump to the first matching tag; with N, jump to the Nth matching tag
`ts[elect][!] [tagstring]`	List the tags that match *tagstring*, using the information in the tags file(s)

Tag commands—vi

Command	Function

`^]`
`g <LeftMouse>`
`CTRL-<LeftMouse>`
	Look up the location of the identifier under the cursor in the `tags` file and move to that location; the current location is automatically pushed to the tag stack

`^T`	Return to the previous location in the tag stack, i.e., pop off one element

Edit-Compile Speedup

Vim provides several commands to increase programmer productivity.

Program development commands—ex

Command	Function
cc[!] [n]	Display error *n* if supplied; otherwise, redisplay the current error
cf[ile][!] [errorfile]	Read the error file and jump to the first error
clast[!] [n]	Display error *n* if supplied; otherwise, display the last error
cl[ist][!]	List the errors that include a filename
[N]cn[ext][!]	Display the Nth next error that includes a filename
[N]cp[revious][!]	Display the Nth previous error that includes a filename
crewind[!] [n]	Display error *n* if supplied
cq[uit]	Quit with an error code so that the compiler won't compile the same file again; intended primarily for the Amiga compiler
mak[e] [arguments]	Run make, based on the settings of several options as described in the next table, then go to the location of the first error

Program development options

Option	Value	Function
errorformat	%f:%l:\ %m	A description of what error messages from the compiler look like; this example value is for gcc, the C compiler from the GNU Compiler Collection
makeef	/tmp/vim##.err	The name of a file that will contain the compiler output; the ## causes Vim to create unique filenames
makeprg	make	The program that handles the recompilation
shell	/bin/sh	The shell to execute the command for rebuilding your program

Option	Value	Function
shellpipe	2>&1| tee	Whatever is needed to cause the shell to save both standard output and standard error from the compilation in the error file

Programming Assistance

Vim provides multiple mechanisms for finding identifiers that are of interest.

Identifier search commands—ex

Command	Function
che[ckpath][!]	List all the included files that couldn't be found; with the !, list all the included files.
[range]dj[ump][!] [count] [/]pattern[/]	Like [^D and] ^D, but search in range lines; the default is the whole file.
[range]dl[ist][!] [/]pattern[/]	Like [D and]D, but search in range lines; the default is the whole file.
[range]ds[earch][!] [count] [/]pattern[/]	Like [d and]d, but search in range lines; the default is the whole file.
[range]dsp[lit][!] [count] [/]pattern[/]	Like ^W d and ^W ^D, but search in range lines; the default is the whole file.
[range]ij[ump][!] [count] [/]pattern[/]	Like [^I and] ^I, but search in range lines; the default is the whole file.
[range]il[ist][!] [/]pattern[/]	Like [I and]I, but search in range lines; the default is the whole file.
[range]is[earch][!] [count] [/]pattern[/]	Like [i and]i, but search in range lines (the default is the whole file). Without the slashes, a word search is done; with slashes, a regular expression search is done.

Command	Function
[*range*]isp[lit][!] [*count*] [/]*pattern*[/]	Like ^W i and ^W ^I, but search in *range* lines; the default is the whole file.

Identifier search commands—vi

Command	Function
[d	Display the first macro definition for the identifier under the cursor
]d	Display the first macro definition for the identifier under the cursor, but start the search from the current position
[D	Display all macro definitions for the identifier under the cursor; filenames and line numbers are displayed
]D	Display all macro definitions for the identifier under the cursor, but start the search from the current position
[^D	Jump to the first macro definition for the identifier under the cursor
] ^D	Jump to the first macro definition for the identifier under the cursor, but start the search from the current position
^W d ^W ^D	Open a new window showing the location of the first macro definition of the identifier under the cursor; with a preceding count, find the specified occurrence of the macro
[i	Display the first line that contains the keyword under the cursor
]i	Display the first line that contains the keyword under the cursor, but start the search at the current position in the file; this command is most effective when given a count
[I	Display all lines that contain the keyword under the cursor; filenames and line numbers are displayed
]I	Display all lines that contain the keyword under the cursor, but start from the current position in the file
[^I	Jump to the first occurrence of the keyword under the cursor

Command	Function
] ^I	Jump to the first occurrence of the keyword under the cursor, but start the search from the current position
^W i ^W ^I	Open a new window showing the location of the first occurrence of the identifier under the cursor; with a preceding count, go to the specified occurrence

Extended matching commands—vi

Provide a preceding count to these commands to move forward or backward by more than one instance of the desired search text.

Command	Function
%	Extended to match the /* and */ of C comments and the C preprocessor conditionals (#if, #endif, etc.)
[(	Move to the Nth previous unmatched (
[)	Move to the Nth next unmatched)
[{	Move to the Nth previous unmatched {
[}	Move to the Nth next unmatched }
[#	Move to the Nth previous unmatched #if or #else
]#	Move to the Nth next unmatched #else or #endif
[*, [/	Move to the Nth previous unmatched start of a C comment, /*
]*,]/	Move to the Nth next unmatched end of a C comment, */

Indentation and formatting options

Option	Function
autoindent	Simple-minded indentation; uses that of the previous line
smartindent	Similar to autoindent, but is smarter about C syntax; deprecated in favor of cindent

Option	Function
cindent	Enables automatic indenting for C programs and is quite smart; C formatting is affected by the rest of the options listed in this table
cinkeys	Input keys that trigger indentation options
cinoptions	Options that tailor your preferred indentation style
cinwords	Keywords that start an extra indentation on the following line
formatoptions	A number of single-letter flags that control several behaviors, notably how comments are formatted as you type them
comments	Describes different formatting options for different kinds of comments, both those with starting and ending delimiters, as in C, and those that start with a single symbol and go to the end of the line, such as in a Makefile or shell program

Folding and Unfolding Text

Folding is enabled with the foldenable option. There are six folding methods, controlled by the foldmethod option, as follows:

diff
    Folds are used for unchanged text.

expr
    Folds are defined by a regular expression.

indent
    Folds are defined by the indentation of the text being folded and the value of shiftwidth.

manual
    Folds are defined using regular Vim commands (such as the search and motion commands).

marker

>Folds are defined by predefined markers (which you can change) in the text.

syntax

>Folds are defined by the syntax of the language being edited.

Folding commands—ex

Command	Function
range fo[ld]	Create a fold for the lines in *range*.
range foldc[lose][!]	Close folds in *range*. With !, close all folds; otherwise, open just one fold.
[*range*] folddoc[losed] *command*	(Fold do closed.) Similar to the g (global) command, this command marks all lines that are in a closed fold and executes *command* on them.
[*range*] foldd[oopen] *command*	(Fold do open.) Similar to the g (global) command, this command marks all lines not in a closed fold and executes *command* on them.
range foldo[pen][!]	Open folds in *range*. With !, open all folds; otherwise, open just one fold.

Folding commands—vi

Folding commands start with z, since it looks something like a folded piece of paper, viewed from the side.

Command	Function
za	Toggle folding. On an open fold, close one or *count* folds. On a closed fold, open folds and set `foldenable`.
zA	Like za, but open or close folds recursively.
zc	Close one or *count* folds under the cursor.
zC	Close all folds under the cursor.
zd	Delete the fold under the cursor. Nested folds are moved up a level. **Careful!** This can delete more than you expect, and there is no undo.
zD	Delete folds recursively starting under the cursor.
zE	Eliminate all folds in the window.
zf *motion*	Create a fold.
zF	Create a fold for *count* lines (like zf).
zi	Toggle the value of `foldenable`.
zj	Move down to start of next fold or down *count* folds.
zk	Move up to start of previous fold or up *count* folds.
zm	Fold more by subtracting one from `foldlevel` if it's greater than zero; set `foldenable`.
zM	Close all folds, set `foldlevel` to zero, and set `foldenable`.
zn	Fold "none": reset `foldenable` and open all folds.
zN	Fold "normal": set `foldenable` and restore all folds to their previous states.
zo	Open one or *count* folds.
zO	Open all folds under the cursor.
zr	Reduce folding. Adds one to `foldlevel`.
zR	Open all folds and set `foldlevel` to the highest fold level.
zv	Open enough folds to make the line with the cursor visible (view the cursor).
zx	Update folds by undoing manually opened and closed folds, reapplying `foldlevel`, and doing zv.

Command	Function
zX	Undo manually opened and closed folds, then re-apply foldlevel.
[z	Move to start of current open fold. If already there, move to start of containing fold if there is one; otherwise, fail. With *count*, repeat the given number of times.
]z	Like [z, but move to the end of the fold or the end of the containing fold.

Folding options

Option	Default
foldclose (fcl)	0
foldcolumn (fdc)	0
foldenable (fen)	foldenable
foldexpr (fde)	0
foldignore (fdi)	#
foldlevel (fdl)	0
foldlevelstart (fdls)	−1
foldmarker (fmr)	{{{,}}}
foldmethod (fdm)	manual
foldminlines (fml)	1
foldnestmax (fdn)	20
foldopen (fdo)	block,hor,mark,per cent,quickfix,search,tag,undo
foldtext (fd)	foldtext()

Insertion Completion Facilities

Vim provides *completion* facilities: the ability to enter only a part of the final text and have Vim provide you with a list of suggested completions based on the commands you use and the content of the current files.

The completion commands (except for completion with the **complete** option) are two-keystroke combinations that start with CTRL-X. Most second keystrokes are not bound to actions in input mode, so it is often useful to map the second keystroke to the original combination, such as `:inoremap ^F ^X^F`.

The completion commands present a list of choices that you can cycle through using CTRL-N and CTRL-P (for "next" and "previous," respectively). Use CTRL-E to end the completion without making a choice, and use CTRL-Y or ENTER to select the current choice and insert it.

The completion facilities are not simple, but they bring considerable power and time savings to long editing sessions. It is worthwhile to invest time to learn to use them. See Chapter 14 of *Learning the vi and Vim Editors (http://oreilly.com/catalog/9780596529833/)* for the details.

Completion commands—vi

The order here is alphabetic by keystroke. Commands marked with a ✓ allow use of the second character to move to the next candidate, along with the regular CTRL-N.

Completion with the **complete** option is the most customizable and flexible method.

Command	Completion	Description
^N ^P	Using complete	Do completion searching forward (^N) or backward (^P), based on the comma-separated list of *completion sources* given in the complete option. The next table lists the possible sources. Use ^X ^N or ^X ^P to copy additional words from the original source.
^X ^D ✓	Macro names	Search the current and included files for macros (defined with #define) that match the text under the cursor. Repeating the command after an insertion

Command	Completion	Description
		copies additional words from the original source.
^X ^F ✓	Filename	Look for filenames (not file contents) that match the word under the cursor. The path option is not used here.
^X ^I	Keyword in file and included files	Similar to keyword completion (^X ^N), but search in included files as well, as specified by the include option; the default is a pattern matching C and C++ #include directives. The path option acts as a search path to find included files in addition to looking in the "standard" places. Repeating the command after an insertion copies additional words from the original source.
^X ^K ✓	Dictionary	Search the files in the comma-separated list that is the value of the dictionary option for a word that matches.
^X ^L ✓	Whole line	Search backward in the file for a line matching what you've typed so far. Typing ^X ^L after inserting a matched line lets you select one of the lines next to the original line that was inserted.
^X ^N ✓ ^X ^P ✓	Keyword in file	Search forward (^X ^N) or backward (^X ^P) for a "keyword" matching what you've typed so far. Keywords are contiguous sequences of the characters appearing in the iskeyword option. Repeating the command after an insertion copies additional words from the original source.
^X ^O ✓	Omni	Call the Vim function named by the omnifunc option to do completion. This function is expected

Command	Completion	Description
		to be filetype-specific (Javascript, HTML, C++, etc.) and loaded when the file is loaded.
^X ^S ✓ ^X s	Spelling	Offer possible spelling corrections for the word under the cursor. Spellchecking must be enabled with the spell option.
^X ^T ✓	Thesaurus	Similar to dictionary completion; search files in the thesaurus option and provide completion from all matching lines. Here, all words on a line with a match are shown as completion options, not just the first word on the line. Similarly, all lines with a possible match are shown.
^X ^U ✓	User function	Call the Vim function named by the completefunc option to do completion.
^X ^V ✓	ex command line	Provide completion for Vim commands. This is intended to simplify Vim script development. Repeating the command does additional completion.
^X ^] ✓	Tag	Search forward in the current and included files for the first tag matching the word under the cursor. If showfulltag is set, Vim displays the tag and the search pattern used for it.

The next table describes possible completion sources for use with the complete option. Sources are listed alphabetically. The default value for complete is ".,w,b,u,t,i".

Name	Description
. (period)	The current buffer.
b	Other buffers, even those that are not loaded in a window (visible).
d	The current and included files; search for macro definitions.
i	The current and included files.
k	The dictionary files listed in the dictionary option.
kfile	Scan file for dictionary lines that match. May be given multiple times, e.g., k~/french. A pattern may be used.
kspell	Use the current spellchecking scheme.
s	The thesaurus files listed in the thesaurus option.
sfile	Scan file for thesaurus lines. May be given multiple times, e.g., s~/french. A pattern may be used.
t,]	Tag completion.
u	The unloaded buffers in the buffer list.
U	The buffers that are not in the buffer list.
w	Buffers in other windows.

Completion options

Option	Default
complete (cpt)	.,w,b,u,t,i
completefunc (cfu)	
completeopt (cot)	menu,preview
define (def)	^\s*#\s*define
dictionary (dict)	
include (inc)	^\s*#\s*include
infercase (inf)	noinfercase
isfname (isf)	@,48-57,/,.,-,_,+,,,#,$,%,~,=
iskeyword (isk)	@,48-57,_,192-255
omnifunc (ofu)	

Option	Default
pumheight (ph)	0
showfulltag (sft)	noshowfulltag
spell	nospell
thesaurus (tsr)	

Diff Mode

When invoked as either vimdiff or gvimdiff, Vim provides *diff mode*, which lets you view a comparison of the differences between two files. vimdiff is for use on a standard terminal (or inside a terminal emulator), while gvimdiff uses the GUI facilities of your operating system.

When Vim is built from source, vimdiff and gvimdiff are usually installed as links to Vim. On a system using a package manager, you may have to install them separately.

Figure 1 shows an example screenshot of gvimdiff in action. The figure shows the salient points:

- Lines that are identical are folded so that they are hidden (see "Folding and Unfolding Text" on page 41 for information on folding text).

- Lines that appear in one file but not in the other are highlighted (in light blue) in the file in which they are present and are shown as lines of dashes in the file from which they are absent.

- Lines that are different between the files are highlighted (in pink), with the actual differences between the lines highlighted in red.

This mode makes it straightforward to move bits of text from one version of a file to another. For example, if you maintain a project using copies of library files from another source, when the source files are revised, it is easy to copy and paste the changes into your version of the file.

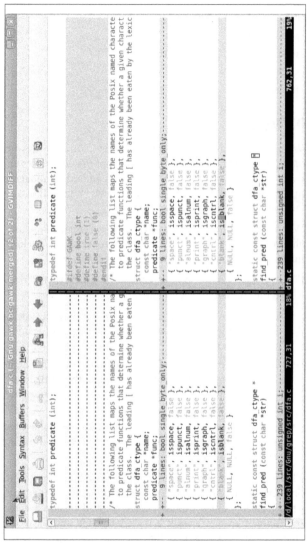

Figure 1. gvimdiff in action

Vim Scripting

Scripting in Vim is a large topic, one deserving of a full book to itself. This section presents some of the barest essentials. For more information, see Chapter 12 of *Learning the vi and Vim Editors (http://oreilly.com/catalog/9780596529833/)* and the online help.

Vim provides essentially a full-featured programming language with variables, operators, control flow constructs, and the ability to define your own functions. This section looks (briefly) at each of these in turn.

Following **vi**, comments start with a double-quote character and continue to the end of the line. Typically you put comments on lines by themselves to avoid problems with double-quoted strings, which are also part of Vim's language.

Variables, options, and numbers

Vim lets you define your own variables and includes a mechanism to indicate the *scope*, or lifetime, of a variable. You may also access the value of Vim options. Variable names consist of any number of letters, digits, or underscores, and may not start with a digit. Vim uses special markers in front of the variable or option name to indicate the type and scope. By default, variables are global:

Prefix	Meaning
&	Vim option
$	Environment variable
@	Register (single-character names)
a:	Function argument
b:	Local to the buffer
g:	Global
l:	Local to the function
s:	Local to script read with **source**
t:	Local to the tab page

Prefix	Meaning
v:	Vim-defined global variable
w:	Local to the window

Two commands assign a value to a variable or remove a variable:

Command	Function
let	Assign a value
unlet[!]	Remove a variable; adding ! prevents a diagnostic if the variable doesn't exist

Numeric values in Vim are always integer values. Prefix a number with 0 (zero) to indicate it is octal (base 8), or with either 0x or 0X to indicate that it is hexadecimal (base 16). Otherwise, the number is taken as decimal (base 10).

Vim provides regular arrays (termed *lists*) and associative arrays (termed *dictionaries*). As dictionaries may hold functions, you can even do object-oriented programming! See the online help for more information.

Control flow commands

The control flow commands are conventional, as described in the following table.

Command	Function
if *condition* *commands* elsif *condition* *commands* else *condition* *commands* endif	If-then-else statement. The elsif and else parts are optional, and there may be as many elsif parts as needed.
for *var* in *list* *commands* endfor	Loop over a list of values, setting variable *var* to a new value each time before running *commands*. This is similar to the shell for loop.

Command	Function
while *condition* *commands* endwhile	While *condition* is true, execute *commands*.

try
  commands
catch *pattern*
  commands
finally
  commands
endtry
	Catch exceptions (see the online help for details).

break	Break out of the enclosing while loop, skipping the rest of the loop body and terminating the loop.
continue	Go to the top of the enclosing while loop, skipping the rest of the loop body.
finish	Exit from a script read with the source command.
throw *expr*	Evaluate *expr* and throw the result as an exception; the exception is caught with a catch clause inside try...endtry.

Operators

Expressions are built up by applying operators to values. Values are obtained from numeric or string constants and from variables, options, and list or dictionary elements. Most of the operators will be familiar to programmers, and their precedence is generally that of the C language ("The usual precedence is used," says the online help).

Operators	Meaning
+ -	Addition and subtraction
* / %	Multiplication, division, and modulus
. (period)	String concatenation
e1 ? *e2* : *e3*	The C ternary operator: if *e1* is true, use *e2*, otherwise, use *e3*
== !=	Equals and not equals
< <=	Less than and less than or equals

Operators	Meaning
> >=	Greater than and greater than or equals
=~ !~	Matches and does not match (regular expression matching)
=	Absolute assignment; use with let
+= -= .=	Incremental assignment: add to, subtract from, and concatenate onto the end; use with let

By default, the comparison operators (==, !=, <, <=, >, >=, =~, !~) ignore case or respect it based on the setting of the **ignorecase** option. Suffixing the operators with # forces the test to match case, whereas using ? forces the test to ignore case.

User-defined functions

Vim lets you define your own functions. The following table outlines the commands related to defining and calling functions, with explanation following the table.

Command	Function
function Name([args]) commands return value endfunction	Define a function
function Name([args]) range commands return value endfunction	Define a function that operates upon a range of lines
function! Name([args]) commands return value endfunction	Define a function, even if the function already exists
function Name(args, ...) commands return value endfunction	Define a function that takes a variable number of arguments
function	List all user-defined function names and their arguments

Command	Function
function *Name*	Display the body of function *Name*
delfunction *Name*	Remove (undefine) function *Name*
[*N*,*M*] call *Func*([*args*])	Call a function upon a range of lines *N* through *M*

User-defined function names *must* begin with an uppercase letter so that Vim can distinguish them from built-in functions.

Arguments (parameters) are optional. If they're supplied, you reference them within the function body using the **a:** prefix on their names. When the "**...**" syntax is used, you access the additional, unnamed arguments as **a:1**, **a:2**, and so on. **a:0** is a count of the additional parameters, and **a:000** is a list of all the additional arguments. Functions using "**...**" may have up to 20 additional arguments.

Functions defined with the **range** syntax are called once for the range of lines; the starting and ending line numbers are available as **a:firstline** and **a:lastline**, respectively. Functions defined without **range** are called once for each line in the range.

Use the **return** statement to return a value from the function. Return values must be numeric; **return** without a value or "falling off the end" of the function causes the function to return zero.

Variables used within a function body are automatically local to the function; you must use the **g:** prefix to access global variables.

The function body is checked for validity when the function is called, not when it's defined. You should therefore test your functions carefully before publishing them.

The **call** command calls a function on a range of lines. Otherwise, function calls may be used as elements in an expression in any context that accepts an expression (such as with **if**).

Vim also provides *function references*, which are variables that "point" at functions and may be used to call them indirectly.

Such variables must also have names that start with an upper-case letter. When combined with dictionaries, they provide a rudimentary object-oriented programming capability; see the online help for the details.

Of course, as is often the case in the Free Software and open source worlds, chances are good that someone else has already written a function that does what you need (or 90% of it). There are many Vim functions available at the Vim website (*http://www.vim.org*). Check there first before diving in to write a function of your own!

Running scripts

There are multiple ways to run scripts. You can read a file directly with the **source** command. For example, your ~/.vimrc file might execute **source** ~/.exrc. Doing this lets you keep commands that will only work in **vi** in the .exrc file, while still letting you execute them in Vim as well.

More commonly used, the *auto-commands* mechanism lets you read and execute scripts based on a file's type, as determined by the file's suffix. For example, the author has the following in his .vimrc file:

```
autocmd BufReadPre,FileReadPre *.xml source ~/.ex-sgml-rc
```

The aliases and input mappings specific to XML are kept in a separate file. This keeps them from getting in the way when you are working on other kinds of files, but makes them available when you are editing XML.

Vim set Options

Option	Default
autoread (ar)	noautoread
background (bg)	dark or light
backspace (bs)	0
backup (bk)	nobackup

Option	Default
backupdir (bdir)	.,~/tmp/,~/
backupext (bex)	~
binary (bin)	nobinary
cindent (cin)	nocindent
cinkeys (cink)	0{,0},:,0#,!^F,o,O,e
cinoptions (cino)	
cinwords (cinw)	if,else,while,do,for,switch
comments (com)	
compatible (cp)	cp; nocp when a .vimrc file is found
completeopt (cot)	menu,preview
cpoptions (cpo)	aABceFs
cursorcolumn (cuc)	nocursorcolumn
cursorline (cul)	nocursorline
define (def)	^\s*#\s*define
directory (dir)	.,~/tmp,/tmp
equalprg (ep)	
errorfile (ef)	errors.err
errorformat (efm)	(too long to print)
expandtab (et)	noexpandtab
fileformat (ff)	unix
fileformats (ffs)	dos,unix
formatoptions (fo)	Vim default: tcq; vi default: vt
gdefault (gd)	nogdefault
guifont (gfn)	
hidden (hid)	nohidden
hlsearch (hls)	nohlsearch
history (hi)	Vim default: 20; vi default: 0
icon	noicon
iconstring	
include (inc)	^\s*#\s*include

Option	Default
incsearch (is)	noincsearch
isfname (isf)	@,48-57,/,.,-,_,+,,,,#,$,%,~,=
isident (isi)	@,48-57,_,192-255
iskeyword (isk)	@,48-57,_,192-255
isprint (isp)	@,161-255
makeef (mef)	/tmp/vim##.err
makeprg (mp)	make
modifiable (ma)	modifiable
mouse	
mousehide (mh)	nomousehide
paste	nopaste
ruler (ru)	noruler
secure	nosecure
shellpipe (sp)	
shellredir (srr)	
showmode (smd)	Vim default: smd; vi default: nosmd
sidescroll (ss)	0
smartcase (scs)	nosmartcase
spell	nospell
suffixes	*.bak,~,.o,.h,.info,.swp
taglength (tl)	0
tagrelative (tr)	Vim default: tr; vi default: notr
tags (tag)	./tags,tags
tildeop (top)	notildeop
undolevels (ul)	1000
viminfo (vi)	
writebackup (wb)	writebackup

nvi—New vi

nvi is a vi clone created for the 4.4BSD Berkeley Unix release. It's intended to be "bug-for-bug" compatible with the original, although it does have a number of extensions over the original vi.

Important Command-Line Options

-c *command*
> Execute *command* at startup.

-F Don't copy the entire file when starting to edit.

-R Start in read-only mode, setting the **readonly** option.

-s Enter batch (script) mode. This is only for **ex** and is intended for running editing scripts. Prompts and nonerror messages are disabled.

-S Run with the **secure** option set, disallowing access to external programs.

nvi Window Management Commands

Command	Function
bg	Hide the current window
di[splay] b[uffers]	Display all buffers, including named, unnamed, and numeric buffers
di[splay] s[creens]	Display the filenames of all backgrounded windows
Edit *filename*	Edit *filename* in a new window
Edit /tmp	Create a new window editing an empty buffer; /tmp is interpreted specially to create a new temporary file
fg *filename*	Uncover *filename* into the current window
Fg *filename*	Uncover *filename* in a new window; the current window is split

Command	Function
Next	Edit the next file in the argument list in a new window
Previous	Edit the previous file in the argument list in a new window
resize ±nrows	Increase or decrease the size of the current window by *nrows* rows
Tag *tagstring*	Edit the file containing *tagstring* in a new window

The ^W command cycles between windows, top to bottom. The :q and ZZ commands exit the current window.

You may have multiple windows open on the same file. Changes made in one window are reflected in the other.

nvi Extended Regular Expressions

You use :set extended to enable extended regular expression matching:

| | Indicates alternation. The left and right sides don't need to be single characters.

+ Matches one or more of the preceding regular expressions. This is either a single character or a group of characters enclosed in parentheses.

? Matches zero or one occurrence of the preceding regular expression.

(...)
    Used for grouping, to allow the application of additional regular expression operators.

{...}
    Describes an interval expression (interval expressions were defined in "Vim Extended Regular Expressions" on page 32).

When extended isn't set, use \{ and \}.

When **extended** is set, you should precede the above metacharacters with a backslash in order to match them literally.

Command-Line History and Completion Options

Option	Description
cedit	The first character of this string, when used on the colon command line, provides access to the command history; pressing ENTER on any given line executes that line.
filec	The first character of this string, when used on the colon command line, does shell-style filename expansion; when this character is the same as for the **cedit** option, command-line editing is performed only when the character is entered as the first character on the colon command line.

Both of these options are not set by default. Set them in your $HOME/.nexrc file.

Tag Stacks

nvi provides both **ex** and **vi** commands for managing the tag stack.

Tag commands—ex

Command	Function
di[splay] t[ags]	Display the tag stack
ta[g][!] *tagstring*	Edit the file containing *tagstring* as defined in the **tags** file
Ta[g][!] *tagstring*	Just like :**tag**, except that the file is edited in a new window
tagp[op][!] *tagloc*	Pop to the given tag or to the most recently used tag if no *tagloc* is supplied
tagt[op][!]	Pop to the oldest tag in the stack, clearing the stack in the process

Tag commands—vi

Command	Function
^]	Look up the location of the identifier under the cursor in the tags file and move to that location; the current location is automatically pushed to the tag stack
^T	Return to the previous location in the tag stack

nvi 1.79 set Options

Option	Default
backup	
cdpath	Environment variable $CDPATH or current directory
cedit	
comment	nocomment
directory (dir)	$TMPDIR, or /tmp
extended	noextended
filec	
iclower	noiclower
leftright	noleftright
lock	lock
octal	nooctal
path	
recdir	/var/tmp/vi.recover
ruler	noruler
searchincr	nosearchincr
secure	nosecure
shellmeta	~{[*?$`'"\
showmode (smd)	noshowmode
sidescroll	16
taglength (tl)	0
tags (tag)	tags /var/db/libc.tags /sys/kern/tags

Option	Default
tildeop	notildeop
wraplen (wl)	0

elvis

elvis is a vi clone written by Steve Kirkendall.

Important Command-Line Options

-a   Load each file named on the command line to a separate window.

-c *command*

    Execute *command* at startup (POSIX version of the historical +*command* syntax).

-f *filename*

    Use *filename* for the session file instead of the default name.

-G *gui*

    Use the given interface. The default is the termcap interface. Other choices include x11, windows, curses, open, and quit. Not all the interfaces may be compiled into your version of elvis.

-i   Start editing in input mode instead of in command mode.

-o *logfile*

    Redirect the startup messages out to a file, instead of stdout/stderr. This is of critical importance to MS Windows users because Windows discards anything written to standard output and standard error.

-R   Start editing each file in read-only mode.

-s   Read an ex script from standard input and execute (per the POSIX standard). This bypasses all initialization scripts.

-S   Set the option **security=safer** for the whole session, not just execution of **.exrc** files. This adds a certain amount of security, but should not necessarily be trusted blindly.

-SS

Set the option **security=restricted**, which is even more paranoid than **security=safer**.

-V   Output more verbose status information.

-?   Print a summary of the possible options.

elvis Window Management

elvis provides multiwindow editing.

Window management commands—ex

Command	Function
close	Close the current window; the buffer that the window was displaying remains intact
new	Create a new empty buffer and create a new window to show that buffer
qall	Issue a :q command for each window; buffers without windows are not affected
sa[ll]	Create a new window for any files named in the argument list that don't already have a window
sl[ast]	Create a new window, showing the last file in the argument list
sne[w]	Same as new
sn[ext] [*file...*]	Create a new window, showing the next *file* in the argument list
sN[ext]	Create a new window, showing the previous file in the argument list
sp[lit] [*file*]	Create a new window; load it with *file* if supplied; otherwise, the new window shows the current file

Command	Function
sre[wind][!]	Create a new window, showing the first file in the argument list; reset the "current" file as the first with respect to the :next command
sta[g][!] *tag*	Create a new window, showing the file where the requested *tag* is found
wi[ndow] [*target*]	With no *target*, list all windows; the possible values for *target* are described in the next table
wquit	Write the buffer back to the file and close the window; the file is saved whether or not it has been modified

Arguments to the :window command

Argument	Meaning
+	Switch to the next window, like ^W k
++	Switch to the next window, wrapping like ^W ^W
-	Switch to the previous window, like ^W j
- -	Switch to the previous window, wrapping
num	Switch to the window whose windowid = *num*
buffer-name	Switch to the window editing the named buffer

Window management commands—vi

Command	Function
^W c	Hide the buffer and close the window
^W d	Toggle the display mode between "normal" and the buffer's usual display mode; this is a per-window option
^W j	Move down to the next window
^W k	Move up to the previous window
^W n	Create a new window and a new buffer to be displayed in the window
^W q	Save the buffer and close the window
^W s	Split the current window

Command	Function
^W S	Toggle the wrap option; this option controls whether long lines wrap or whether the whole screen scrolls to the right, and is a per-window option
[N] ^W ^W	Move to the next window, or to the Nth window
^W]	Create a new window, then look up the tag underneath the cursor
^W +	Increase the size of the current window (termcap interface only)
^W -	Reduce the size of the current window (termcap interface only)
^W \	Make the current window as large as possible (termcap interface only)

elvis Extended Regular Expressions

\| Indicates alternation.

\+ Matches one or more of the preceding regular expressions.

\? Matches zero or one of the preceding regular expressions.

\@ Matches the word under the cursor.

\= Indicates where to put the cursor when the text is matched.

\(...\)

Used for grouping to allow the application of additional regular expression operators.

\{...\}

Describes an interval expression (interval expressions were defined in "Vim Extended Regular Expressions" on page 32).

POSIX bracket expressions (character classes, etc.; see "POSIX character classes" on page 15) are available.

Command-Line History and Completion Movement Keys

Key	Effect
↑, ↓	Page up and down through the Elvis ex history buffer
←, →	Move around on the command line

Insert characters by typing and erase them by backspacing over them.

You can use the TAB key for filename expansion.

To get a real tab character, precede it with a ^V. Disable filename completion entirely by setting the Elvis ex history buffer's **inputtab** option to **tab** via the following command:

```
:(Elvis ex history)set inputtab=tab
```

Tag Stacks

elvis provides both **ex** and **vi** commands for managing the tag stack.

Tag commands—ex

Command	Function
ta[g][!] [*tagstring*]	Edit the file containing *tagstring* as defined in the **tags** file
stac[k]	Display the current tag stack
po[p][!]	Pop a cursor position off the stack, restoring the cursor to its previous position

Tag commands—vi

Command	Function
^]	Look up the location of the identifier under the cursor in the **tags** file and move to that location; the current location is automatically pushed onto the tag stack
^T	Return to the previous location in the tag stack

Edit-Compile Speedup

elvis provides several commands to increase programmer productivity.

Program development commands—ex

Command	Option	Function
cc[!] [*args*]	ccprg	Run the C compiler; useful for recompiling an individual file
er[rlist][!] [*file*]		Move to the next error's location
mak[e][!] [*args*]	makeprg	Recompile everything that needs recompiling (usually via **make**)

Display modes

Mode	Display appearance
hex	An interactive hex dump, reminiscent of mainframe hex dumps; good for editing binary files
html	A simple web page formatter; the tag commands can follow links and return to the starting web page
man	Simple manpage formatter; like the output of **nroff -man**
normal	No formatting; display text as it exists in the file
syntax	Like **normal**, but with syntax coloring turned on
tex	A simple subset of the T_EX formatter

Display-mode commands—ex

Command	Function
di[splay] [*mode* [*lang*]]	Change the display mode to *mode*; use *lang* for syntax mode
no[rmal]	Same as :display normal, but much easier to type

Options for print management

Option	Function
lpcolor (lpcl)	Enable color printing for PostScript and MS Windows printers
lpcolumns (lpcols)	The printer's width
lpcontrast (lpct)	Control shading and contrast; for use with the lpcolor option
lpconvert (lpcvt)	If set, convert Latin-8 extended ASCII to PC-8 extended ASCII
lpcrlf (lpc)	The printer needs <CR><LF> to end each line
lpformfeed (lpff)	Send a formfeed after the last page
lplines (lprows)	The length of the printer's page
lpoptions (lpopt)	Control of various printer features; this matters only for PostScript printers
lpout (lpo)	The file or command to print to
lptype (lp)	The printer type
lpwrap (lpw)	Simulate line wrapping

Values for the lptype option

Name	Printer type
bs	Overtyping is done via backspace characters; this setting is the closest to traditional Unix nroff
cr	Line printers; overtyping is done with carriage return
dumb	Plain ASCII; no font control
epson	Most dot-matrix printers; no graphic characters supported

Name	Printer type
hp	Hewlett-Packard printers and most non-PostScript laser printers
ibm	Dot-matrix printers with IBM graphic characters
pana	Panasonic dot-matrix printers
ps	PostScript; one logical page per sheet of paper
ps2	PostScript; two logical pages per sheet of paper

elvis 2.2 set Options

elvis 2.2 has a total of 225 options that affect its behavior. The most important ones are summarized here. Options shared with vi are not repeated here.

Option	Default
autoiconify (aic)	noautoiconify
backup (bk)	nobackup
binary (bin)	
boldfont (xfb)	
bufdisplay (bd)	normal
ccprg (cp)	cc ($1?$1:$2)
directory (dir)	
display (mode)	normal
elvispath (epath)	
equalprg (ep)	fmt
focusnew (fn)	focusnew
font (fnt)	
gdefault (gd)	nogdefault
home (home)	$HOME
italicfont (xfi)	
locked (lock)	nolocked
lpcolor (lpcl)	nolpcl
lpcolumns (lpcols)	80

Option	Default
lpcrlf (lpc)	nolpcrlf
lpformfeed (lpff)	nolpformfeed
lpheader (lph)	nolph
lplines (lprows)	60
lpout (lpo)	
lptype (lpt)	dumb
lpwrap (lpw)	lpwrap
makeprg (mp)	make $1
prefersyntax (psyn)	never
ruler (ru)	noruler
security (sec)	normal
showmarkups (smu)	noshowmarkups
sidescroll (ss)	0
smartargs (sa)	nosmartargs
spell (sp)	nospell
taglength (tl)	0
tags (tagpath)	tags
tagstack (tsk)	tagstack
undolevels (ul)	0
warpback (wb)	nowarpback
warpto (wt)	don't

vile—vi like Emacs

vile is a vi clone based originally on MicroEmacs, whose main goal is to provide the "finger feel" of vi.

Important Command-Line Options

-g N

> vile begins editing on the first file at the specified line number; this can also be given as +N.

-h   Invokes vile on the help file.

-R   Invokes vile in "read-only" mode; no writes are permitted while in this mode.

-s pattern

> In the first file, vile executes an initial search for the given pattern; this can also be given as +/pattern.

-v   Invokes vile in "view" mode; no changes are permitted to any buffer while in this mode.

-?   vile prints a short usage summary and exits.

@ cmdfile

> vile runs the specified file as its startup file and bypasses any normal startup file.

vile Window Management Commands

Command	Key sequences	Function
delete-other-windows	^O, ^X 1	Eliminate all windows except the current one
delete-window	^K, ^X O	Destroy the current window unless it's the last one
edit-file, E, e find-file	^X e	Bring given (or under-cursor, for ^X e) file or existing buffer into window
grow-window	V	Increase the size of the current window by *count*
move-next-window-down	^A ^E	Move next window down (or buffer up) by *count* lines
move-next-window-up	^A ^Y	Move next window up (or buffer down) by *count* lines

Command	Key sequences	Function
move-window-left	^X ^L	Scroll window to left by *count* columns, half-screen if *count* unspecified
move-window-right	^X ^R	Scroll window to right by *count* columns, half-screen if *count* unspecified
next-window	^X o	Move to the next window
position-window	z *where*	Reframe with cursor specified by *where*, as follows: center (., M, m), top ([ENTER], H, t), or bottom (-, L, b)
previous-window	^X O	Move to the previous window
resize-window		Change the current window to *count* lines
restore-window		Return to window saved with save-window
save-window		Mark a window for later return with restore-window
scroll-next-window-down	^A ^D	Move next window down by *count* half-screens
scroll-next-window-up	^A ^U	Move next window up by *count* half-screens
shrink-window	v	Decrease the size of the current window by *count* lines
split-current-window	^X 2	Split the window in half; a *count* of 1 or 2 determines which becomes current
view-file		Bring given file or existing buffer into window; mark it "view-only"
historical-buffer	_	Display a list of the first nine buffers; a digit moves to the

Command	Key sequences	Function
		given buffer, _ _ moves to the most recently edited file
toggle-buffer-list	*	Pop up/down a window showing all the vile buffers

vile Extended Regular Expressions

\| Indicates alternation.

\+   Matches one or more of the preceding regular expressions.

\?   Matches zero or one of the preceding regular expressions.

\s \S

Matches whitespace and nonwhitespace characters, respectively.

\w \W

Matches "word-constituent" characters (alphanumerics and the underscore, "_") and nonword-constituent characters, respectively.

\d \D

Matches digits and nondigits, respectively.

\p \P

Matches printable and nonprintable characters, respectively. Whitespace is considered to be printable.

\(...\)

Provides grouping for *, \+, and \?, as well as making matched subtexts available in the replacement part of a substitute command.

vile allows the escape sequences \b, \f, \r, \t, and \n to appear in the replacement part of a substitute command. They stand for backspace, formfeed, carriage return, tab, and newline, respectively. Also, from the vile documentation:

Note that vile mimics perl's handling of \u\L\1\E instead of vi's. Given :s/\(abc\)/\u\L\1\E/, vi will replace with abc whereas vile and perl will replace with Abc. This is somewhat more useful for capitalizing words.

Command-Line History and Completion

vile stores all your ex commands in a buffer named [History]. Options control your access to it and the use of the minibuffer (the colon command line).

History commands—vi

Key	Meaning
↑, ↓	Move up (previous), down (more recent) in the history
←, →	Move left, right on the recalled line
BACKSPACE	Delete characters

The ex command line provides completion of various sorts. Completion applies to built-in and user-defined vile commands, tags, filenames, modes, and variables, and to the terminal characters (the character setting, such as backspace, suspend, and so on, derived from your stty settings).

History options

Option	Meaning
history	Log commands from the colon command line in the [History] buffer.
mini-edit	The character that toggles the editing mode in the minibuffer to use vi motion commands. You can also use the vi commands i, I, a, and A.
mini-hilite	Define the highlight attribute to use when the user toggles the editing mode in the minibuffer. The value should be one of none, underline, bold, italic, or reverse; the default is reverse.

Tag Stacks

vile provides both ex and vi commands for managing the tag stack.

Tag commands—ex

Command	Function
ta[g][!] [*tagstring*]	Edit the file containing *tagstring* as defined in the tags file
pop[!]	Pop a cursor position off the stack, restoring the cursor to its previous position
next-tag	Continue searching through the tags file for more matches
show-tagstack	Create a new window that displays the tag stack; the display changes as tags are pushed to or popped off the stack

Tag commands—vi

Command	Function
^]	Look up the location of the identifier under the cursor in the tags file and move to that location; the current location is automatically pushed to the tag stack
^T ^X ^]	Return to the previous location in the tag stack, i.e., pop off one element
^A ^]	Same as the :next-tag command

Edit-Compile Speedup

Unlike the other clones, vile only provides vi commands for increasing programmer productivity.

Program development commands—vi

Command	Function
^X ! command ENTER	Run *command*, saving the output in a buffer named [Output]
^X ^X	Find the next error; vile parses the output and moves to the location of each successive error

The error messages are parsed using regular expressions in the buffer [Error Expressions]. vile creates this buffer automatically and uses it when you use ^X ^X. You can add expressions to it as needed.

You can point the error finder at an arbitrary buffer (not just the output of shell commands) using the :error-buffer command. This lets you use the error finder on the output of previous compiler or **egrep** runs.

vile 9.8 set Options

Option	Default
alt-tabpos (atp)	noatp
animated	animated
autobuffer (ab)	autobuffer
autocolor (ac)	0
autosave (as)	noautosave
autosavecnt (ascnt)	256
backspacelimit (bl)	backspacelimit
backup-style	off
bcolor	default
byteorder-mark (bom)	auto
check-access	current
check-modtime	nocheck-modtime
cindent	nocindent
cindent-chars	:#{}()[]

Option	Default
cmode	off
color-scheme (cs)	default
comment-prefix	^\s*\(\(\(\s*[#*>]\)\)|\(///*\)\)\)\+
comments	^\s*/\?\(\(\s*[#*>/]\)\)\+/\?\s*$
cursor-tokens	regex
dirc	nodirc
dos	nodos
fcolor	default
fence-begin	/*
fence-end	*/
fence-if	^\s*#\s*if
fence-elif	^\s*#\s*elif\>
fence-else	^\s*#\s*else\>
fence-fi	^\s*#\s*endif\>
fence-pairs	{}()[]
file-encoding	auto
filtername (fn)	
for-buffers (fb)	mixed
glob	!echo %s
highlight (hl)	highlight
history (hi)	history
ignoresuffix (is)	\(\.orig|~\)$
horizscroll (hs)	horizscroll
linewrap (lw)	nolinewrap
maplonger	nomaplonger
meta-insert-bindings (mib)	mib
mini-hilite (mh)	reverse
modeline	nomodeline
modelines	5
overlap-matches	overlap-matches

Option	Default
percent-crlf	50
percent-utf8	90
popup-choices (pc)	delayed
popup-msgs (pm)	nopopup-msgs
recordseparator (rs)	lf[a]
resolve-links	noresolve-links
reuse-position	noreuse-position
ruler	noruler
showchar (sc)	noshowchar
showformat (sf)	foreign
showmode (smd)	showmode
sideways	0
tabinsert (ti)	tabinsert
tagignorecase (tc)	notagignorecase
taglength (tl)	0
tagrelative (tr)	notagrelative
tags	tags
tagword (tw)	notagword
undolimit (ul)	10
unicode-as-hex (uh)	nounicode-as-hex
unprintable-as-octal (uo)	nounprintable-as-octal
visual-matches	none
xterm-fkeys	noxterm-fkeys
xterm-mouse	noxterm-mouse
xterm-title	noxterm-title

a This depends on the platform for which vile is compiled.

Internet Resources for vi

There are many resources and items of interest on the Internet related to **vi** and its clones. This section provides a brief overview of some of them:

http://www.thomer.com/vi/vi.html
> Thomer M. Gil's *vi Lover's Home page*. This is one of two main sites for **vi**, with links to many resources and other sites.

http://www.vi-editor.org
> Sven Guckes's *VI Pages*. This is the second of the main **vi** sites.

http://www.darryl.com/vi.shtml
> A "This site is vi powered" logo, as shown in Figure 2.

http://www.cafepress.com/geekcheat/366808
> Concise **vi** command references, printed on coffee mugs, t-shirts, and more!

http://www.networkcomputing.com/unixworld/tutorial/009/009.html
> A nine-part tutorial on **vi** by Walter Zintz, originally published in *Unix World* magazine.

http://ars.userfriendly.org/cartoons/?id=20000106
> This is the start of the "vigor" story line in the *User Friendly* comic strip, which was the inspiration for the next item in this list.

http://vigor.sourceforge.net
> The source code for **vigor**.

Figure 2. vi powered!

Program Source and Contact Information

Editor	Modernized, original vi
Author	Gunnar Ritter
Email	*gunnarr@acm.org*
Source	*http://ex-vi.sourceforge.net*
Editor	Vim
Author	Bram Moolenaar
Email	*Bram@vim.org*
Source	*http://www.vim.org/*
Editor	nvi
Author	Keith Bostic
Email	*bostic@bostic.com*
Source	*https://sites.google.com/a/bostic.com/keithbostic/nvi*
Editor	elvis
Author	Steve Kirkendall
Email	*kirkenda@cs.pdx.edu*
Source	*ftp://ftp.cs.pdx.edu/pub/elvis/README.html*
Editor	vile
Authors	Kevin Buettner, Tom Dickey, and Paul Fox
Email	*vile@nongnu.org*
Source	*http://www.invisible-island.net/vile/vile.html*

Index

We'd like to hear your suggestions for improving our indexes. Send email to
index@oreilly.com.